Annie Fields

The Singing Shepherd

And Other Poems

Annie Fields

The Singing Shepherd
And Other Poems

ISBN/EAN: 9783744704441

Printed in Europe, USA, Canada, Australia, Japan

Cover: Foto ©Thomas Meinert / pixelio.de

More available books at **www.hansebooks.com**

THE SINGING SHEPHERD

AND OTHER POEMS

BY

ANNIE FIELDS

BOSTON AND NEW YORK
HOUGHTON, MIFFLIN AND COMPANY
The Riverside Press, Cambridge
1895

Copyright, 1895,
By ANNIE FIELDS.

All rights reserved.

The Riverside Press, Cambridge, Mass., U.S.A.
Electrotyped and Printed by H. O. Houghton & Co.

> E tu figliol, che per la mortal pondo
> Ancor giù tornerai, apri la bocca
> E non asconda quel ch' io non ascondo.
>
> PARADISO, Canto xxvii.

Of song may all my dwelling be full, for neither is sleep more sweet, nor sudden spring, nor are flowers more delicious to the bees, so dear to me are the Muses.

THEOCRITUS.

CONTENTS.

	PAGE
THE SINGING SHEPHERD	1
THE COMFORTER	4
GIVE	7
WAITING	9
CEDAR MOUNTAIN	10
THE FUTURE SUMMER	12
THE FIRST THANKSGIVING DAY AFTER THE WAR	16
A SOLDIER'S MOTHER	19
TEN YEARS AFTER	20
BLUE SUCCORY	24
ANDANTE	25
THE RETURN	27
COMPENSATION	29
DEFIANCE	30
"SONG, TO THE GODS, IS SWEETEST SACRIFICE"	31
CHILDREN	32
LITTLE GUINEVER	34
THE RUINED HOME	36
CHANGING SKIES	39
THE POET'S CHOICE	40
ELIZABETH'S CHAMBER	42
THE SONG-SPARROW	44

CONTENTS.

HERB YARROW	45
A MEMORY OF INTERLACHEN	47
MIDSUMMER NOON	48
UPON REVISITING A GREEN NOOK	49
SWEETBRIER	50
THE BEE AND THE ROSE	51
UNCHANGED	52
PERDITA	53
THE SEVENTH SLEEPER	54
SILENCE AND SOLITUDE	56
ON A WHARF	58
ON WAKING FROM A DREAMLESS SLEEP	60
SONG	62
SPRINGTIME	63
NEMESIS	64
IN MIST AND DARK	66
THE WING OF FAITH	68
THE PRODIGAL'S RETURN	70
CHRYSALIDES	71
THE BIRD OF AUTUMN	73
THE PATRIOT'S BIRTHPLACE	74
THE MESSAGE	76
GRETCHEN IN EXILE	77
TO ——	79
"THE HOUR YE KNOW NOT"	82
THE GIFT DIVINE	83
TO THE DWELLERS IN HOUSES	84
PREPARATION	86
A DREAM IN MAY	88
LET US BE PATIENT	89
TO L. W. J.	91

CONTENTS.

PARTED	92
ENDYMION	94
WINTER LILACS	95
THE CRICKET	98
THE OFFERING	99
TO ONE WHOSE SIGHT WAS FAILING	100
THE GARDEN OF FAME	101
IN MEMORIAM	103
MIDNIGHT	105
A FAR HAVEN	107
THE HAUNTS OF POESY	109
THE FOLDING	111
TIDES	112
THE SOUL OF THE POET	113
HOME	114
ROS SOLIS	115
SACRED PLACES	117
KYPRIS	118
TO THE CHILDREN	120
MORTALITY	121
PERMANENCE	122
THE WARDER	124
ON THE DEATH OF A YOUNG GIRL	126
THE PASSING OF TENNYSON	127
COMATAS	128
A FALLING STAR	130
THE POET'S HOUSE	131
TO ——, SLEEPING	134
THE MYSTERIES OF ELEUSIS	135
REVERY OF ROSAMOND IN HER BOWER	138
C. T.	140

THE CORONAL	142
THE TRAVELER	144
UPON A MASK OF AN UNKNOWN WOMAN'S FACE	145
"STILL IN THY LOVE I TRUST"	147
THE RIVER CHARLES	148
FLAMMANTIS MŒNIA MUNDI	151
"A THOUSAND YEARS IN THY SIGHT"	152
DEATH, WHO ART THOU?	153

THE SINGING SHEPHERD.

TO A POET'S MEMORY.

THE shepherd climbed the hill through dark and light,
    And on and on he went,
    Higher and higher still,
Seeking a pasture hidden in the height.
    He followed by the rill,
    He followed past the rocks,
And as he went singing he shepherded his flocks.

How wide those upland pastures none e'er knew;
    But over the wild hills
    A stretch of watered grass,
Outspreading, though half hidden from the view,
    Invites that all may pass.
    He sees the weary way,
Yet, while the shepherd sings, how brief the toilsome day!

Stand thou with me and watch his eager feet.
  He stays not for the drought,
  Nor lingers in the shade,
Save where the clover and the streamlet meet;
  There, quiet, unafraid,
  The tender lambs may feed
While the calm noon gives rest to those who are in need.

Again I see his figure cut the sky,
  Then sink, and reappear
  Upon a loftier plain,
Where far beneath his feet the eagles cry.
  I cannot hear his strain,
  But in a moving drift
I see the snow-white sheep follow the music's lift.

The climbing shepherd long ago has passed,
  Yet in the morning air,
  For those who listen well,
His song still lingers where his feet made haste;
  And where his music fell
  The happy shepherds know
His song allures them yet beyond the fields of snow.

THE SINGING SHEPHERD.

O climbing shepherd, I would follow thee!
    Over the dizzy heights,
    Beyond the lonely pass,
Thy piping leads; the path I always see!
    I see thee not, alas!
    Because of death's rude shock;
Yet thou, dear shepherd, still art shepherding thy flock.

THE COMFORTER.

MY heart is searching for thee,
    And lost in longing for thy voice!
Voice that lies deeper than the permanent sea,
Deeper than thought,
Deeper than my own life.

Behold the child,
With yellow locks and aspect wild,
Gazing on nought;
With hands hung listless,
And heart at strife,
Waiting, a young lost Israelite,
For angels' food!

We are all children lost, of one great race,
Sighing for light,
Whom thou alone canst bless;

Give us manna, the promised good!
Show us thy face!
Else how should joy survive
The ebbing tide,
And hear the burden of the desert sea?

Where art thou, Guide?
Ah! where dost thou abide?
Within what heart or on what wave dost live?
Must man forever hunger till beyond his reach
Splendors of speech
Fall on his untaught ear?
Give me new light!
Give me new day!

"Who are ye
 Thus crying for the light of a new day?
 If wonders press on thee,
 Delay thy feet, — delay!
 But now
 Fear clouds thy brow,
 And seems to hunt thee through the wood.
 Listen, delay!
 I, the comforter, am near;

I am the loveliness of the earth;
I am the spring's birth;
I sing on the solemn shore;
I am the presence at the dark, low door."

GIVE.

"The vine shall give her fruit, and the ground shall give her increase, and the heavens shall give their dew."

THE fire of freedom burns,
    Her flame shall reach the heaven;
Heap up the sacred urns,
And life for life be given!

Woman of nerve and thought,
Bring in the urn your power!
By you is manhood taught
To meet the supreme hour.

Come with your sunlit life,
Maiden of gentle eye!
Bring to the gloom of strife
Light by which heroes die.

GIVE.

Give, rich men, proud and free,
Your children's costliest gem!
For Liberty shall be
Your heritage to them.

O friend with heavy urn,
What offering bear you on?
The figure did not turn:
I heard a voice, "My son."
　1862.

WAITING.

Drop, falling fruits and crispëd leaves,
    Ye ring a note of joy for me:
Through the rough wind my soul sails free,
High over waves that Autumn heaves.

I watch the crimson maple-boughs;
I know by heart each burning leaf,
Yet would that like a barren reef
Stripped to the breeze those arms uprose!

Under the flowers my soldier lies!
Yet come, thou chilling pall of snow,
Lest he should hear who sleeps below
How, yet in bonds, the captive cries!

Fade swiftly then, thou lingering year,
Test with the storms our eager powers;
For chains are broken with the hours,
And Freedom waits upon thy bier.
    December, 1862.

CEDAR MOUNTAIN.

RING the bells, nor ring them slowly;
  Toll them not,—the day is holy!
Golden-flooded noon is poured
In grand libation to the Lord.

No mourning mothers come to-day
Whose hopeless eyes forget to pray;
They each hold high the o'erflowing urn,
And bravely to God's altar turn.

Ye limners of the ancient saint!
To-day another virgin paint;
Where with the lily once she stood
Show now the new beatitude.

To-day a mother crowned with pain,
Of silver beauty beyond stain,

Clasping a flower for our land,
A sheathëd lily in her hand.

Each pointed leaf, with sword-like strength,
Guarding the flower throughout its length;
Each sword has won a sweet release
To the flower of beauty and of peace.

Ring the bells, nor ring them slowly,
To the Lord the day is holy;
To the young dead we consecrate
These lives that now we dedicate.
   1862.

THE FUTURE SUMMER.

SUMMER in all! deep summer in the pines,
    And summer in the music on the sands,
And summer where the sea-flowers rise and fall
About the gloomy foreheads of stern rocks.

Can mockery be hidden in such guise!
To peep, like sunlight, behind shifting leaves,
And dye the purple berries of the field,
Or gleam like moonlight upon juniper,
Or wear the gems outshining jeweled pride!
Can mockery do this, and we endure
In Nature's rounded palace of the world?

Where, then, has fled the summer's wonted peace?
Sweeter than breath borne on the scented seas
Over fresh fields and brought to weary shores,
She should await the season's worshiper;

But as a star shines on the daisy's eye,
So shines our conscience on the face of peace,
And lends a calmer lustre with the dew;
When that star dims, the paling floweret fades!

Yet there be those who watch a serpent crawl,
And, blackening, sleep within a blossom's heart,
Who will not slay, but call their gazing "peace."
Even thus within the bosom of our land
Creeps, serpent-like, Sedition, and hath gnawed
In silence while a timid crowd stood still.

O suffering land! O dear, long-suffering land,
Slay thou the serpent ere he sting the core!
Take thou our houses and amenities;
Take thou the hand that parting clings to ours,
And, going, bears our heart into the fight;
Take thou, but slay the serpent ere he kill!

Now, as a lonely watcher on the strand,
Hemmed by the mist and the quick-coming waves,
Hears but one voice, the voice of warning bell,
That solemn speaks, "Beware the jaws of death!"

Death on the sea and warning on the strand! —
Such is our life, while summer, mocking, broods.

O mighty heart! O brave, heroic soul!
Hid in the dim mist of the things that be,
We call thee up to fill the highest place!
Whether to till thy corn and give the tithe,
Whether to grope, a picket, in the dark,
Or, having nobly served, to be cast down,
And, unregarded, passed by meaner feet,
Or, happier thou, to snatch the fadeless crown,
And walk in youth and beauty to God's rest, —
The purpose makes the hero, meet thy doom!

We call to thee, where'er thy pillowed head
Rests lonely for the brother who has gone,
To fix thy gaze on freedom's chrysolite,
Which rueful fate can neither crack nor mar;
And, hand in hand indissolubly bound
To thy next fellow, hand and purpose one,
Stretch thus, a living wall, from the rock coast
Home to our ripe and yellow heart of the West,
Impenetrable union triumphing.

The solemn autumn comes, the gathering-time!
Stand we now ripe, a harvest for the right!
That, when fair summer shall return to earth,
Peace may inhabit all her sacred ways;
Lap in the waves upon melodious sands,
And linger in the swaying of the corn,
Or sit with clouds upon the ambient skies, —
Summer and peace brood on the grassy knolls
Where twilight glimmers over the calm dead,
While clustered children chant heroic tales.

    October, 1864.

THE FIRST THANKSGIVING DAY AFTER THE WAR.

HOLY silence of Thanksgiving!
   With the presence of the living,
With the peace the season takes,
Falling with the falling snowflakes,
After the harrowing dissonance
And sorrowing of wars!

Where the spruces droop their arms
Heavy with deep weight of snow,
Lured and beckoned by their charms
Through a winding path we go,
Leading to the cottage stoop
Where awaits warm salutation
From the merry household group,
Shining with young love's elation.
The crackling fire, the merry dance,
And the stories of adventure

And what patriots endure;
And the lady brings a chart,
Worn and crumpled in the service,
Spreads it on her silken dress,
While her slender fingers press
Reverently each warworn part
As to heal some piteous crevice;
Then, brown curls to brown curls bent
In lovers' measureless content,
He guides her hand (but does not speak)
From Baltimore to Cedar Creek.

Here was the end, brave heart!
His words burst forth like gusts of rain
Washing across an April sky,
Bringing a penetrating pain.
But — young was their life's ecstasy,
And death in friendship hath no part,
And noble memories will bless
And crown their happiness:
Therefore they spoke as he were here once more,
Nor marked a silent vision cross the floor, —
The vision of a woman kneeling,
Her baby's little arms, appealing,

Stretched toward that ragged sheet
Which knowledge made complete,
Watching with look of rapt beatitude
Those others in the selfsame attitude
She and her sleeping lover knew
Before his spirit flew.

The bride arose to fold the page
Grown sacred with the look of age;
The winds were gathering; through the storm
Again I saw the flitting form
Watch where the merry voices rise,
Seeing calm joy in married eyes,
And then — a marriage chamber in a tent —
The past with a high future blent.

Saw the Norway spruces bending,
Saw their snowy arms extending
Over a wind-strewn bed
Where lay her valiant dead,
And saw her turn with the disconsolate who weep
Over the form asleep.
    1865.

A SOLDIER'S MOTHER.

M. L. P.

HER words the hope of nations crown,
    And stir brave boyhood with their leaven,
        Her patriot fire
        Wakes noble ire,
She wastes in gracious deeds, like one
Whose heart is on the fields of heaven.

Far on some viewless height her eyes
Behold another scene than ours;
        She drops no tear,
        She feels no fear,
But beckons weeping mothers rise
And walk with her in unseen bowers.
   1864.

TEN YEARS AFTER.

EASTER SUNDAY.

THE Sunday morn was fresh and clear,
    The Sunday bells rang cheerly out,
The old New England church was near
And welcomed faith or doubt.

There was room even for such as I
Who took the hospitable grace
Of one who lonely sat, hard by
The door, and gave me place.

She was a matron in life's prime,
Sitting alone in her high-backed pew,
Daughter of old New England time,
Mother of ages new.

She gave — 't was all she had to give ! —
Her last young boy for her country's good,
And now she would as cheerful live
As with her darling brood.

A crown for his young life is won,
Wrought out of slavery's broken chain;
His few glad days in glory done,
Set without cloud or stain.

His work unfinished is her work;
His fame invested is his form;
No solitude can ever lurk
Where love grows ever warm.

Therefore she sits within her pew,
And views her baby's lowly seat,
And where, as older still he grew,
He chafed his restless feet.

Rough figures scratched with tiny hands
Remain upon the high pew walls,
Soldiers perhaps in uncouth bands,
Or wandering childish scrawls.

And still she sits and notes them all,
Dear relics of her vanished day;
Nor do we see her tear-drops fall,
Nor watch them wiped away.

She looks upon the joy that was,
As herald of the joy to be;
She weighs the glory that he has
Against the things we see, —

And fills the vessel of the state
With all she owns of wealth and hope,
Patient, content to work and wait
Through life's appointed scope, —

Until, until, she knows not where
Nor how, but once again she sees
Her dear ones, and may then declare
Upon her bended knees: —

"Those few short days were not in vain:
My soldier died upon the field,
But through earth's maze of loss and gain
I bravely bore his shield."

And thus she sits within her pew
Calmly, nor lets the tear-drops fall,
While we with brimming eyelids view
Those tracings on the wall.
  1863-1873.

BLUE SUCCORY.

IN WAR TIME.

ONLY the dusty common road,
    The glaring weary heat;
Only a man with a soldier's load,
    And the sound of tired feet.

Only the lonely creaking hum
    Of the cicada's song;
And a broken fence where tall weeds come
    With spikëd fingers strong.

Only a drop of the heaven's blue
    Left in a wayside cup, —
A cup of joy for the plodding few
    And eyes that look not up.

Only a weed to the passer-by,
    Growing among the rest;
Yet something clear as the light of the sky
    It lodges in my breast.

ANDANTE.

BEETHOVEN'S SIXTH SYMPHONY.

SOUNDING above the warring of the years,
    Over their stretch of toil and pain and fears,
        Comes the well-loved refrain,
        The ancient voice again.

Sweeter than when, beside the river's marge,
We lay and watched, like innocence at large,
        The changeful waters flow,
        Speaks this brave music now.

Tender as sunlight upon childhood's head,
Serene as moonlight upon childhood's bed,
        Comes the remembered power
        Of that long-vanished hour.

The river ran with merry voice and low,
The gentle ripples rippling far below,

Talked with no idle voice,
Though idling were their choice.

Now through the tumult and the pride of life,
Gentler, yet firmly soothing all its strife,
  Nature draws near once more
  And knocks at the world's door:

She walks within her wild harmonious maze,
Weaving her melodies from doubt and haze,
  And leaves us freed from care
  Like children standing there.

THE RETURN.

THE bright sea washed beneath her feet,
   As it had done of yore,
The well-remembered odor sweet
   Came through her opening door.

Again the grass his ripened head
   Bowed where her raiment swept;
Again the fog-bell told of dread,
   And all the landscape wept.

Again beside the woodland bars
   She found the wilding rose,
With petals fine and heart of stars, —
   The flower our childhood knows.

And there, before that blossom small,
   By its young face beguiled,
The woman saw her burden fall,
   And stood a little child.

She knew no more the weight of love,
  No more the weight of grief;
So could the simple wild-rose move
  And bring her heart relief.

She asked not where her love was gone,
  Nor where her grief was fled,
But stood as at the great white throne,
  Unmindful of things dead.

COMPENSATION.

IN the strength of the endeavor,
  In the temper of the giver,
In the loving of the lover,
  Lies the hidden recompense.

In the sowing of the sower,
In the fleeting of the flower,
In the fading of each hour,
  Lurks eternal recompense.

DEFIANCE.

CLOTHO, Lachesis, Atropos!
   All your gain is not my loss;
Spin your black threads if you will;
Twist them, turn, with all your skill;
Hold! there's one you cannot sever!
One bright thread shall last forever.

You are defied, you, Atropos!
Draw your glittering shears across, —
One still mocks your cruel art!
From the fibres of my heart
Did I spin the shining thread
That will live when you are dead.

Fate, but hark! one thing I'll teach:
There are wonders past your reach,
Of the heart and of the soul:
Woman's love's past your control!
These are not threads of your spinning,
No, nor shall be of your winning.

"SONG, TO THE GODS, IS SWEETEST SACRIFICE."

"BEHOLD another singer!" Criton said,
    And sneered, and in his sneering turned the leaf:
"Who reads the poets now? They are past and dead,
Give me for their vain work unrhymed relief."
A laugh went round. Meanwhile the last ripe sheaf
Of corn was garnered, and the summer birds
Stilled their dear notes, while autumn's voice of grief
Rang through the fields, and wept the gathered herds.

Then in despair men murmured: "Is this all, —
To fade and die within this narrow ring?
Where are the singers, with their hearts aflame,
To tell again what those of old let fall, —
How to decaying worlds fresh promise came,
And how our angels in the night-time sing."

CHILDREN.

WE cannot know the child's deep heart,
　　We cannot learn his grief;
Though childhood still is dear to man,
And the spent time so brief.

Who knew the hours of silent joy
In our green garden plot,
Those mornings with the hollyhocks,
Whose beauty fadeth not! —

Days when the hidden steps of spring
Were heard, not understood;
When music from afar swept in,
Born of her dreamful mood, —

Seasons when young Love hid his face
Through joyless, restless days;
The winter of the growing soul,
When summer but delays.

Who knew how sad the darksome path,
The hour of grief how long!
Nor how there came the strong bright day,
And through the mist a song.

LITTLE GUINEVER.

"When Queen Guinever of Britain was a little wench."
                                    LOVE'S LABOR 'S LOST.

SWIFT across the palace floor
    Flashed her tiny willful feet;
"Playfellow, I will no more,
    Now I must my task complete."

Arthur kissed her childish hand,
    Sighed to think her task severe,
Walked forth in the garden land,
    Lonely till she reappear.

She has sought her latticed room,
    Overlooking faery seas,
Called Launcelot from a bowery gloom
    To feast of milk and honey of bees.

"Had we bid Prince Arthur too,
    He had shaken his grave head,

Saying, 'My holidays are few!' —
  May queens not have their will?" she said.

Thus she passed the merry day,
  Thus her women spake and smiled:
"All we see we need not say,
  For Guinever is but a child."

THE RUINED HOME.

AT nightfall, coming from the wood,
    I crossed the hilltop's gloomy brow,
Where one unsheltered farmhouse stood,
    Neglected, dark, and low.

No lamp announced a breathing soul;
    The chimney's blue, reluctant thread
Alone betrayed a living coal
    Of life, all else seemed dead.

At length, observing curiously
    And gazing back as on I went,
One little pale face I could see
    Close to the window bent.

And in my mind I saw all night
    That child's face watching by the pane;
Once more I passed that weary height
    And lingered there again.

THE RUINED HOME.

At dawn I rose, and, walking forth,
  Met one who toiled upon the road,
Morning or evening nothing loth
  With talk to ease his load.

He told me that he knew when first
  The sunshine played across that floor,
And the bright buds of spring-time burst
  Around that household door, —

And gayer than the buds of spring,
  More musical than summer birds,
The songs a happy wife would sing
  'Mid lowing of the herds.

Swift are the steps that lead to ill,
  Friendly the sparkling cup appears,
And idlers share the bowl until
  The scene must end in tears.

Hour after hour his passion grew;
  Quickly the power of will can cease;
Haunted by dreadful shapes, he knew
  No more the days of peace.

She watched him till the arms of death
    Laid her upon the earth's calm breast.
May not her love and prayers have breath
    To bring him into rest?

Now day and night the little maid,
    His only child, scarce ten years old,
Still watches, never once afraid
    Of darkness nor of cold.

The morning sun was brave and gay
    And birds were filling earth with song,
While yet my heart pursued that way,
    That rocky hill of wrong.

I saw the child beside the pane
    Still gazing on the clouded sky;
Her solitude was mine again,
    And mine her agony.

CHANGING SKIES.

UPON the noontide's perfect blue
    There sleeps a perfect cloud;
The lily's faultless form is hid
Within her leafy shroud.

The cloud lets fall her silver wing
And fades the perfect blue;
The lily's form betrays a fault —
Alas, love! art thou true?

THE POET'S CHOICE.

TO dwell all day upon the mountain height,
    And ride all night upon the rifted cloud;
To watch the earliest arrow in his flight
Morning despatches from her misty shroud;
To lie at evening on the lonely sands,
Hearing the waters tell mysterious tales
Of whispering lovers upon unknown strands,
And suns that die to gladden rosier sails;
To wander in the midnight of the wood,
And hear the timid cuckoo cry afar;
To watch the rising of June's flowery flood,
And Hesper leading evening with one star, —

These are the poet's joy, the singer's food;
Yet often from the mighty top of song,
Where, clothed with solitude, his feet have stood,
He gazes wistful from the awful throng

Of shapes imagination hath made his
Down to the fireside and the homely bliss
Of one returning and the greeting kiss.

The throbbing stars return, why should not he?
Why ever float upon the restless sea?
Open thy heart, love, let me fly to thee!

ELIZABETH'S CHAMBER.

AT AMESBURY.

I ENTERED her half-opened door;
   A welcome like the voice of seas,
When overland their mellow roar
   Comes homeward on the summer breeze,
Gave greeting to my listening heart.
   In vain I crossed the echoing room;
The voice was still a voice apart,
   Though memories ripened into bloom,
Touched by the sacred presence there,
   Pervading perishable things, —
A grace that filled the common air
   With sense of overshadowing wings.
The pendant blossoms fading breathed
   Into new life to speak of her;
The gathered autumn boughs hung wreathed
   To welcome their lost worshiper.
But still she came not; silence dwelt
   And solitude where she abode.

Their dumb lips told the truth I felt:
   Though lonely be the place she trod,
Wide is her radiant chamber now;
   Her spirit gilds the morning cloud,
And lights the day until his brow
   Sinks in the ocean's purpling shroud;
And in the heart of love a bed
   Is laid whereon her sleep is sweet;
There lives she whom the world calls dead,
   There we may kiss her gracious feet.

THE SONG-SPARROW.

CAN you hear the sparrow in the lane
    Singing above the graves? she said.
He knows my gladness, he knows my pain,
    Though spring be over and summer be dead.

His note hath a chime all cannot hear,
    And none can love him better than I ;
For he sings to me when the land is drear,
    And makes it cheerful even to die.

'T is beautiful on this odorous morn,
    When grasses are waving in every wind,
To know my bird is not forlorn,
    That summer to him is also kind, —

But sweeter, when grasses no longer stir
    And every lilac-leaf is shed,
To know that my voiceful worshiper
    Is singing above my voiceless dead.

HERB YARROW.

EVERYWHERE the Yarrow grows!
   Here and there the thistle blows,
Here and there the barberries,
By the brook the plumy fern;
We know where the lily is,
Where the dear wild roses burn:
But the Yarrow everywhere
Wanders on the common air.

No one need to search for thee:
Even now thy leaf I see
Peeping o'er my opened book,
Throwing so fair a shadow down,
So perfect, that I can but look,
And, looking, find new wonder crown
The bliss of beauty which before
Taught my spirit to adore.

In thy bitter odors blent
Health we find, not discontent;
In thy name a tender grief
For that love once drowned in Yarrow,
Stream that never gave relief
To the faithful " winsome marrow."
Bitter Yarrow! Flowing Yarrow!
Still lament thy winsome marrow!

Emblem of our equal land,
Where men and women helpful stand,
And love and labor, high and low;
Type of the low! Thou lovely plant!
Teach the proud-hearted how to know
The sacred worth of Nature's grant,
The strength of bitterness, and the sweet
Humility of beauty's feet.

A MEMORY OF INTERLACHEN.

THERE is a light in darkness which the soul
   Can never know until the sense hath crept
From height to height across the shadowless peaks
Which sentinel thy valley; there are deeps
In thy green hollows, where still thought can lie
Through summer noons unended, glad with dreams;
There, too, is twilight, sudden-black with storm,
When thunder speaks from the unapproachable hills,
And earth shakes at the arrows of his light;
There have I heard a cithern's tinkling sound,
And hollow bursts of laughter from the hall,
While awful thunder shook the world again.
There have I seen pale clouds retreat before
The glory of God's coming, and day die
In lingering splendor on the voiceless Horn;
And while keen players bent around their board
I 've watched the gold of distant stars appear
Circling in music over yon white brows.

MIDSUMMER NOON.

CONFIDENT Summer!
    Thou art here, thou radiant comer;
The sumach and bayberry,
Soft sighing of the sea,
The ever-climbing sun,
The pausing of high noon
When early birds have done —
I know them all! I rest
Upon thy dew-fed breast.
The squirrel questions me,
The oak his acorn drops,
Wild-apple boughs bend over me,
Nor ever stops
The sighing, endless sighing of the sea.

UPON REVISITING A GREEN NOOK.

THE sky is clear, the voice is fresh
    Of waters beating on the shore,
And nature to my heart her heart
    Now lays once more.

Mindful of summer days long past,
    She will not show a weeping face,
But, cheerful with remembered joy,
    Gives gladness place.

The light slips down from other skies
    And mingles with the blue of this;
I hear another music through
    The sparrow's bliss.

The light of an unfading love
    Paints the gay grass and frames the sky,
And hides the moon in morning seas
    And cannot die.

SWEETBRIER.

TENDER of words should singer be,
    Sweetbrier, who would tell of thee;
One who has drunk with eager lip
And treasured thy companionship; —

One who has sought thee far and wide,
In early dew with morning pride;
To whom thou art no new-made friend,
Whose memories on thy breath attend.

For such thou art a lemon grove,
Where wandering orient odors rove;
Yet loyal ever to thy home,
The valley where the north winds roam.

THE BEE AND THE ROSE.

THERE is a constant joy that I have found
   On upland pastures in the light of noon,
Far from a human face or human sound,
That I could tell, were I a golden bee
Like this one who goes booming toward the sea,
Making the most of summer, gone so soon,
And passing on life's way melodiously.

There is an ecstasy that I have known
Among the shadows of green arching things
That I could breathe, if I had only grown
In fragrant beauty like this brier rose,
Which lowly lives and wholly unpraised blows, —
Cheering the bright air where the robin sings,
And only this one simple duty knows!

UNCHANGED.

ONCE men could walk these roads and hear no sound
Save the sad ocean beating on the shore,
Or song of birds who wait not on the roar
  Of waters wrestling with their rocky bound;
  The iris bloomed unseen beside the pool,
The morning rose unmarked, the evening fell
On the broad pastures, and none came to tell
  Other than tales of love in the shadows cool.
  Now with the dawn the cowherd on his way,
The mason and the builder with their tools,
Meet and salute, take counsel of the rules
  To be observed in laboring through the day.
Perchance they never think to hear the voice
That calls forever, has forever called,
And shall forever when these ears are palled;
  Yet for one listener, though the eyes grow dim,
And though the pleasant places are destroyed,
And nooks unveiled whence music was decoyed,
  The great Unchanged still smiles and waits for him.

PERDITA.

ALONE across the silver-fretted skies
    Walked the white moon; attendant wreaths of
        cloud
Wrapt her still steps, and downward to the sea
Her shadowed light descended brokenly;
    A sad and lonely sight unto her eyes
That joyful watched the day-spring's promise proud,
Then saw day fade in dark, and mists enshroud
    The path wherein the pallid moon must rise.

Perdita, standing on the night-black marge,
Gazed down upon the waters' constant change,
Shuddering with fear before that passage strange
    Over the ocean's dark uncertain floor;
She saw no rudder in the waiting barge,
    No beaconing light upon that farther shore.

THE SEVENTH SLEEPER.

BEHOLD him lie in beauty and in vigor,
    The seventh sleeper! all the rest awakened;
Behold the wingèd hours are flitting by him
With flutter, and with music on their pinions!
Beautiful hang the dews beside the highway,
The bitter highway where the sad have fallen;
Beautiful shine the blossoms of the dawning,
But droop their heads before the blaze of noontide,
While yet he sleeps and may not be awakened.
Morning and noonday and the dews of even,
Evening and midnight and the dews of morning,
Find him yet sleeping in the tremulous shadow,
Where oak-leaves whisper to the breeze above him.
Soft are his limbs and white as foam in moonlight,
Nor know they aught of change or earth's decaying,
Since Gabriel, the angel, lifts them often.

We are but shades and wait not the arousing:
Pass on; he must awaken like those others

To find them gone, alas! he knows not whither.
What can avail the beauty of the creature!
All else is born of change; the words are dying,
The youths his childhood knew have passed to silence,
And the old words no longer are remembered.

SILENCE AND SOLITUDE.

GODS of the desert! you are they
    We shun from childhood's earliest breath;
Our passing joys are but your prey;
    You wait the hours from birth to death.

Over soft lawns where blossoms sleep,
    Under warm trees where love was born,
I see your haughty shadows creep,
    And wait to meet you there, forlorn.

Afar on ancient sands you rest,
    Carven in stone, where ancient thought
Wrapt you in terrors, — shapes unblest,
    Dreadful, by might of ages wrought.

But not in Egypt's land alone
    Sleeps the great desert; everywhere
Where gladness lived that now is done,
    Behold a desert of despair!

Strange messengers! your brows of gloom
   Haunt every creature born of earth;
You follow to the darkened room;
   You watch the awful hour of birth.

You show the lovely wayside rose
   Whose antique grace is born anew
To eyes of grief. Grief only knows
   How tender is the sunset's hue.

Gods of the desert! by your hand
   Through the sad waters are we brought
Into a high and peaceful land
   To drink of fountains else unsought.

ON A WHARF.

THE moonlight filled the waters and the strand;
   The floating spires gleamed toward the starry
      land;
Pale Hero seemed upon her Sestian height
   To stand with torch alight.

At anchor slept a heavy rounded keel
Whose moveless rudder made the senses wheel
To music dropping from the Antwerp bells
   In fluctuating swells.

A distant sound blending with dripping oar,
I thought a voice, and then a voice no more,
Past the Armenian convent's solemn wall
   Shot with swift rise and fall.

A stately barge moved on a stately river,
Bearing a queen from happy France forever

To Holyrood, the witness of her shame,
    Her beauty and sad fame.

There stood two lovers over Spezzia's bay,
Silent, enamored of the watery way;
One must soon pass to meet the purple dark
    Borne in yon treacherous bark.

Breathless I watch a noble vessel come
Tented with sail and happy as for home:
Forward she bounds, when swift the moonlit gleam
    Disparts our shadowy dream.

I tread upon my native city's piers;
I see what hope, what loveliness are hers;
Her ships come sailing in unsullied light
    From outer seas to-night.

ON WAKING FROM A DREAMLESS SLEEP.

I WAKED; the sun was in the sky,
　　The face of heaven was fair;
The silence all about me lay,
　　Of morning in the air.

I said, Where hast thou been, my soul,
　　Since the moon set in the west?
I know not where thy feet have trod,
　　Nor what has been thy quest.

Where wast thou when Orion past
　　Below the dark-blue sea?
His glittering, silent stars are gone,
　　Didst follow them for me?

Where wast thou in that awful hour
　　When first the night-wind heard

The faint breath of the coming dawn,
   And fled before the word?

Where hast thou been, my spirit,
   Since the long wave on the shore
Tenderly rocked my sense asleep
   And I heard thee no more?

My limbs like breathing marble
   Have lain in the warm down;
No heavenly chant, no earthly care,
   Have stirred a smile or frown.

I wake; thy kiss is on my lips;
   Thou art my day, my sun!
But where, O spirit, where wast thou
   While the sands of night have run?

SONG.

O PALE and silent dawn, wilt speak to me?
   Above the voice and motion of the sea
      I listen for my love.

O noon of splendor, with thy bird and bee,
And thy face hidden in yon warm pine-tree,
      Knowest thou not my love?

Enchanter thou, O deep and solemn night!
I follow thee, moon-led, through dark and bright
      To find the feet I love.

SPRINGTIME.

I WAKENED to the singing of a bird,
  He was the bird of spring!
And, lo!
At his sweet note
The flowers began to grow,
Grass, leaves, and everything;
As if the green world heard
The trumpet of his tiny throat
From end to end, and winter and despair
Fled at his melody and passed in air.

I heard at dawn the music of a voice;
O my belovëd, then I said, the spring
Can visit only once the waiting year,
The bird can bring
Only the season's song, nor his the choice
To waken smiles or the remembering tear.
But thou dost bring
Springtime to every day, and at thy call
The flowers of life unfold though leaves of autumn
    fall.

NEMESIS.

An evening born for dreams! upon the shore
    Lies the long glory in her vanishing
Of day grown tender ere she is no more;
The light is love's own presence; everything
Is sacred in that joy; nature must sing
Low to herself, her cradle-song! the same
She sang of old and made the meadows sing;
That was when faith was young, — ere unfaith came.

Late lingered, sporting in their world of bliss,
The wingëd creatures bred to haunt the wave;
Ah! who can tell if aught removed from this
Our joy, may be the joys of those who lave
Their wing, and flit upon the marge, and save
Themselves from death, where, toying two by two,
They seek the awful hand that comes to pave
The sandy highways fresh for footprints new.

Sudden the stillness and the rapture end;
Death has rushed in! a shot laid one bird low,

While one, to silence winging, — with no friend, —
In solitude upon his way must go!
The waves are dark; perchance he may not know
His path, for who can know when left alone,
And darkness falls on all, above, below,
Ah! who can know his way when love is gone!

But to the mind that has conceived such death
And brings this misery upon the world,
To him who sees not that the lightest breath
Sacred within the bird or blossom curled
Is bliss, a mystery of life close-furled;
On him whose heart cares not for nature's heart, —
Upon his head one day a bolt is hurled,
And in the death he feared not he has part.

IN MIST AND DARK.

UNFALLEN drops hung on the grass
    And dripped from the bright aster's head;
Voiceless did the swallows pass
Above our voiceless dead.

Crickets to the morning air
Sang the season's evening song,
While the sea-birds' dusky lair
Glimmered with their throng.

Nor other sound, save dropping tears,
Until the distant light-house bell
Across the land, across our fears,
In wide vibrations fell, —

Fell surging over driven ships
That wander blind in dreadful seas,
With music out of iron lips
For women on their knees.

Wild tears, restrain your overflow !
Down to the darkest gulfs that be,
Thus the great voice shall ever go
Across life's fateful sea.

THE WING OF FAITH.

> "L'Aquila
> L 'uccel di Dio."
> *Paradiso.*

O BIRD of God! Unto the saint
    Thou stretchest out thy wing:
Strong in thy strength he will not faint,
But, ever rising, sing.

Strongest of wingëd creatures thou,
Great eagle of our God!
From what vast eyrie bendest now
Where feet have never trod, —

To watch the world of waiting men,
And soothe their tired eyes,
To lift them out of earthly ken
Into thy mysteries?

Where, eagle of the Lord! hast borne —
Into what unknown bliss —

The weary ones from beds of thorn,
The dear ones that we miss?

Out in the dark we follow thee,
We seek the unsetting sun;
What untold glories shall we see
Before the flight be done!

O bird of God! unto the saint
Thou stretchest out thy wing:
Strong in thy strength he shall not faint,
But, ever rising, sing.

THE PRODIGAL'S RETURN.

T IS strange indeed! We wander, we forget,
    We lose ourselves in countless deeds that fret
And trouble the sad hours; then do we turn
And silent sit, like ashes in an urn,
Beside the waters where in youth we strayed.
The Soul, grown timid, of herself afraid,
Comes with no queenly bearing back to seek
The beautiful green courts wherein none speak
Save voices of the air and the deep sea.
She has forgot that Nature made her free
Once in that land divine, and magic tales
Whispered within the stillness of strange sails
That cross at midnight through the moonlit track
Of ocean, and, unnamed, ne'er venture back.

CHRYSALIDES.

NIGHT-BLUE skies of thine,
    Egypt, and thy dead who may not rest,
Who with wide eyes
Stand staring in the darkness of the mine!
Thy woman, Egypt, with her breast
Two cups of carven gold,
And hands that no more rise
In praise or supplication, or to sound
The timbrel in the dance!
White is thy noontide glare,
But no keen glance
Of yet created sun
Can pierce the deeps and caverns of thy dead.
They are overspread
With a new earth, where new men come and go,
And sleep when all is done;
While far below,
Shut from the upper air,
These stirless figures, bound
In awful cerements, must forever wait.

There is another land
Where in a valley once the god Pan slept,
Under the young blue sky, between two peaks;
And here a hero, running, as one seeks
For fame, with ardor which his strength outstepped,
Fell dying in the stillness; quiet lay
The rounded marble limbs in the green grass.
An eagle, pausing on his fiery way,
Down swooped. Lo! as he soared, alas!
Nearing his awful steep,
Where only the dews weep,
And bearing in his clutches that bright form,
He heard the hero's voice:
" Eat, bird, and feed thyself! This morsel choice
Shall give thy claws a span;
This courage of a man
Shall bid thy pinion swell,
And by my strength thy wings shall grow an ell."

THE BIRD OF AUTUMN.

TO ——

LATE bird, who singest now alone
    When woods are silent and the sea
Breathes heavily and makes a moan,
Faint prescience of woe to be, —
A sweetness hovers in thy voice
Spring knows not; autumn is thy choice.

Dear bird, what tender song is thine,
Born out of loss and nursed in storm;
A messenger of grace divine
Enshrouded in thy feathery form!
So com'st thou, darling, with the close
Of summer, lovelier than her rose.

THE PATRIOT'S BIRTHPLACE.

ESSEX, MASSACHUSETTS.

SILENT, breezy afternoons,
   Silent, dull November eves,
Creaking gate and rusty hinge,
Voices of dead leaves.

Summer brings the tansy now,
Flaunting round the ancient well;
Farther stretches web and waste,
Time's decaying spell.

Wide across the continent
Speaks the patriot's deathless word;
Blossoms on the rocky hills,
In the vales is heard.

"I will give the Morning Star
   To him, the Lord saith, who shall keep

My work unfailing to the end,
Nor ever slothful sleep."

Then let winter tempests rage,
And the careless hand of spring
Scatter weeds where'er she goes, —
And autumn ruin bring!

Built up of our larger hope,
Of equal laws and equal right,
His home shall only oceans bind,
Nor ages quench his light.

THE MESSAGE.

TREES, the green trees, rocks, and the wave-
washed sands,
You are all here! while, like the summer birds,
Yet how unlike! the soul of man has passed
Out of his perfect form and vanished quite.
Now question we the rocks and ask the trees
To point the way he went and show us where?
To bring us news of him, while we press on,
Spent with our errands in this nether world.
O trees and rocks, alas! and whispering sands,
I think you bear a message! Let me haunt
Your wild, that in the silence I may lose
Nothing of the great secret you have heard,
And fain would tell if man would pause to hear.

GRETCHEN IN EXILE.

TO HER LOVER.

KIND art thou, and these faces all are kind,
    But in my dreams
I see them not: I see the Neckar wind,
    I see the beams
Of morning dance before my childhood's eye
    On that far sky.

Dost thou remember how each gray stone face
    Peeped from the bed
Of ivy, nature-woven round that place?
    No longer dead,
In some strange, magic hour they seemed to stir
    For their child worshiper.

Dost thou remember where the ripening vine
    O'ertops the wall?
The roadside rest, the flask of golden wine,
    The Alpine call?

Alas! thou canst not; hasten then with me
Back through the darkening sea!

Forever in my dreams must I return!
The kine at rest
I see, afar, where Alpine roses burn;
And I am blest
While lingering beside them! Wake me not,
O darling, wake me not!

TO ——.

"Pain is not the fruit of pain."
               E. B. B.

AFAR! afar! the rosy sails are far,
   And far sound all the voices of the world;
Tenderly hither bends the evening star,
And with an uttered hush the waves are curled;
Thy loneliness hath thrown a viewless bar
Across thy life, as when a storm has hurled
The mountain downward, and the shepherd's track
Is lost, and wearily he wanders back.

Must thou then wander while the years decay
And carry with them hopes that feed the soul?
'T was here the little loves were wont to stray;
Now they have vanished with their laughter droll;
They elsewhere music heard and ran away
Beyond the desert and the greening knoll;
Sweet was their presence, but they pined and fled
Where music, dance, and feasting are not dead.

TO ———.

Dead they are not! earth's gladness cannot die
While still live human hearts who seek to find
Each other, longing to pour forth the sigh
That broods within the breast of all mankind;
Nor while the clouded days go slowly by
And many-handed cares our spirits bind,
Till suddenly Love vanishes and alone
We dwell and listen to his echo, not his tone.

Knowledge by suffering entereth; therefore ye,
Who have lost all, alone can know how dear
The voice which in the silence speaks to me,
Bidding depart the shuddering face of fear.
Companion in earth's grief! the evening sea
Is calmer now for us, the sky more clear;
Over these rosy waves the voice divine
Cries, Comfort ye! this beauty all is Mine!

Mine are the painted petals and the hues
That shine in all things; Mine the power that fills
This empty vessel of the world; the dews
Freshening the grass; the awful flood that spills
From the mountain-top: my messengers infuse
Color and speech in all; and Nature wills

Through gladness of her beauty thus to bring
Man home, where all the fountains of desire spring.

Turn then, and find the consolations borne
In on the lonely spirit from the fields
That fade and die, their loveliness outworn.
Would I could tell the harvest autumn yields!
O ye who sorrow! stand not now forlorn
As envious archers must, deprived of shields!
Ye are the blessëd ones! the heavens rain down
On your sad hearts a joy till now unknown.

Alone indeed ye are, and so must stand:
The desert places will not bloom again;
The frost of winter covers all the land;
The air is only laden with one strain;
The blossoming pastures are now swept with sand,
And everywhere we hear a cry of pain;
Listen! the Word saith: All shall die save thou,
Spirit, who liveth in the Eternal Now.

"THE HOUR YE KNOW NOT."

IN the still night,
   Pallid with moonlight and unstirred by wind,
The noisy waves fell crashing on the sand,
Saying there will be rain.

But he who slept till day, and waked to find
The sheeted raindrops beating on the land,
Did loud complain
His disappointed hope.

Even thus we sleep,
Knowing the moment and the parting near;
We question not of happiness or pain,
Nor in the midnight do we wake to hear
The raindrops feeding earth's wide grassy slope!

THE GIFT DIVINE.

DIVE, O diver, and bring
    A pearl for her throat;
Dip, O fisher, and sing
Lying afloat;
Thus perchance in your net
You may find the magic ring.

Strive, O striver, no more!
When the apple is ripe,
When the south wind blows from the shore,
And the wild-birds pipe,
Late shall the song be yours;
Oh remember, ye who implore!

Beautiful is she and dear:
In vain would you give her
Jewels both rare and clear;
No stream nor river
Shall give you her love
Till the stately planets draw near.

TO THE DWELLERS IN HOUSES.

O SINGERS who tell
    Of the glory of light, the music of leaves, the
        voice of the sea;
And poets who chant of the footstep untrammeled
        and buoyant and free!
The truth is half told!
And the wilderness stands,
Undiscovered and bold.

Forever inviting!
A garden unmeasured, a sweetness unlearned, a music
        unframed;
A lamp to the spirit, a force to the soul, a power un-
        tamed.
Why cleanse we and eat,
Why slumber and drink,
Yet hunger for meat?

Take thine own! and rejoice
In the shade of the oak, in beauty of summer, in fruit
of the vine;
With the birth of the lily, the death of the rose, the
strength of the pine;
Too rich to rehearse!
Though the days were renewed,
And the might of a verse.

Not alone, not alone,
Of these would I sing; the beauty we love, the Love
that endures;
But the waning of days, the falling of leaves, and the
power that cures;
O silence! O day!
Send thy children abroad,
Come winter, come May!

Thou blue bending roof!
We would live, let us live, in the light of the sky!
Here is truth and constancy, here is power that can-
not die!
Open, O nature, thine heart
To these imprisoned ones,
And tell them whose voice thou art!

PREPARATION.

LAY thy heart down upon the warm, soft breast,
    Of June and take thy rest;
The world is full of cares that never cease,
    The air is full of peace.

Lie thou, my heart, beneath the burnished leaves;
    What though the sad world grieves?
Is not the green earth joyous and at play
    Upon this bright June day?

Yet eager dost thou watch the building birds,
    The busy brooding herds,
The pauseless journey of the sunlit days,
    The joy that never stays.

O heart for whom the summer days are bright,
    Wouldst thou, too, gather light?
Art thou astir with every leaf that moves,
    And the first bird that roves?

PREPARATION.

Art thou abroad with the white morning star
    Scaling the heights afar?
Ceaselessly mounting, O thou heart, some hill,
    The springs of life to fill?

As midnight to the dawn, as dark to day,
    As sun and shade at play,
So do the hours exchange and tempests tune
    Their awful harps in June.

This is the hour when buds prepare to break,
    When blossoms fruitage take;
This is the hour of breathing ere the heat
    O'ertake our wearied feet.

A DREAM IN MAY.

A VISION of a quiet place where lay
    Late apple-blossoms scattered on the grass;
A carpet greener far than all the day
Our eyes had seen, alas!

A vision in the night of what shall be!
A rounded hillock and a day of peace,
A tender memory of a soul set free,
Earth greener where we cease.

Such was the quiet place whereon there lay
Pale apple-blossoms scattered on the grass;
A carpet greener far than all that day
Mine eyes had seen, alas!

LET US BE PATIENT.

"Let us be patient."
                OPHELIA.

HEAT overspread the earth, the birds were dumb;
　　A shrouding of white cloud, which was not cloud,
Or mist, which was not mist, half hid the sun
And half betrayed; Sleep poured her drowsy draught
Over the morning eyes of student men,
And all was stirless: yet the day advanced;
There were loud outcries in the market-place;
And busy women hurried to and fro,
Each on her errand, till the evening came.
Then toward the sundown rose a mighty storm
Which roused the sleeping earth, and raging aimless winds
Tore the great seas and ravaged all the land;
Then the impatient spirits whose languid noon
Darkened the sweetness of their summer day
Arose and met the awful feet of the Lord,

Walking the earth and teaching men to know
There shall be times to work and times to wait
We cannot understand, until the hour
When we shall pass the boundary of the sun.

TO L. W. J.

ON HER BIRTHDAY, SEPTEMBER 13, 1878.

WHEN the breath of autumn comes
    First, to say the summer's done,
When the birds their leafy homes
Rifle of the seed and cone,
While the yellow sun lies warm
On the apple and the farm,
And the perfect grass is gay
With hawkweed, as with flowers of May,
When the early morn is bright
And all things wear the tender light
Love wears before it vanisheth, —
I say, dear friend, this is like thee,
So plenteous art thou and so free;
Thy good cheer sorrow banisheth;
And yet a softened gleam doth rest,
Upon thee, for upon thy breast
Many a wintry storm hath pressed;
Soon thou knowest the birds shall cease,
And Love that gave them give thee peace.

PARTED.

"That was and is and ever shall be."

TO A. D. T. W.

THE river sings his ancient song
    Upon his stony bed,
The pine and birch and maple throng
And join with waving head.

O follow, follow up the stream
And rest ye, loving eyes!
There where the mountains like a dream
Fold round the shadowy skies.

O eyes! 'tis but the river's bed
And shivering birch ye see!
Look not to find her pretty head
Beside the gleaming tree.

The hermit-thrush, in hidden ways
Where all but song is dim,

Sings on and on, "Symbolic days,"
And still repeats his hymn.

By night the river's plaint is long,
At noon tall pines complain,
Until I think to these belong
A knowledge of our pain.

ENDYMION.

THE moon was up last night, and all the earth
   Was gay under the favor of her face;
Secure from wandering footsteps, creatures bred
In lonely clefts sped over grassy lawns,
And sniffed strange odors from exotic blooms;
The wilding blossoms gathered, worshiping,
New whiteness from the silver of her beam,
While fairies spread bright yellow canopies
To shield them from the keenness of her eye.
This morn, how tired out do they all appear!
The forehead of the sky now wears a veil,
The winds have ceased, the fairy shields remain,
The borrowed whiteness of the blossom stays;
But silent are they all and hide their love,
Timid as one first touched by lover's glance,
Who stands half slain with all heaven in her heart.

WINTER LILACS.

TO G. D. H.

A BUNCH of lilacs there by the door;
    That and no more!
Delicate, lily-white, like the new snow
    Falling below;
A friend saw the flowers and brought them to me,
    As one who should see
A trifle, a glove, but dropped and returned,
    While a loving thought burned.

Dark all day was that room of mine,
    Till those flowers divine
Into my darkness brought their own light,
    And back to the sight
Of my spirit the happiest days of June
    And the brooklet's tune; —

Where the old front door was left open wide,
    While by my side

One sat, who, raising his eyes from the book
    With the old fond look,
Asked if I loved not indeed that page
    And the words of the sage.

And as we spoke, the cool blue sky,
    The robin nigh,
The drooping blossoms of locust-trees
    Humming with bees,
The budding garden, the season's calm,
    Dropt their own balm.

All these, my friend, were brought back to me,
    Like a tide of the sea,
When out of winter and into my room
    Came summer's bloom:
The flowers reopened those shining gates
    Where the soul waits
Many and many a day in vain,
    While in the rain
We stand, and, doubting the future, at last
    Forget the past.

So you will believe what a posy may do,
    When friends are true,

WINTER LILACS.

For the sick at heart, in the wintry days,
    When nothing allays
The restless hunger, the tears that start,
    The weary smart,
But the old, old love, and the summer hush
    And the lilac bush.

THE CRICKET.

ALL summer long the cricket sings,
    But in June the busy birds,
Proud as youth, on their young wings
Sing above the lowing herds;
Willows whisper to the springs,
All the bright blue air is full
Of music, and our sense is dull.

By and by the birds are still,
By and by the herds withdrawn;
Summer bees have drunk their fill,
Autumn winds the flowers have strewn:
Then the crickets have their will;
Now, we say, is summer done,
Now the crickets have begun.

THE OFFERING.

MY altar holds a constant flame;
    There eager, day by day,
I lay my offering; all the same
In dust it drifts away.

The days return, the seasons turn,
And punctual with the morn
I bring my offering, and I burn
What life from life has torn.

And rarely at the dawn or eve,
And rarely in the night,
Down from the altar I receive
A compensating light.

Therefore in joy I offer still
Myself when day is born;
For late or soon a light will fill
My spirit else forlorn.

TO ONE WHOSE SIGHT WAS FAILING.

> "Count it for certainty,
> Light is with thee bewildered and not dead."
> Dante's *Paradiso*.

DEAR fading eyes! wherefrom the fading sight
　　Falls like the sunset of a falling day,
But leaves no hope that morning's footstep light
Will bring again what Time has taken away!
Dawn, when she mounts afresh on glory's height,
Gladdening anew the valleys of the world,
Must leave thy powers ever in mist enfurled
To wander restless through thy waking night.
Thus pondered I, when, lo! the vale of grief
Burst sudden into song, and all was well.
I watched the vision through a rain of tears
With him who saw therein certain belief:
What saw I? Neither verse nor song can tell
The blessed certainty, the all-seeing spheres.

THE GARDEN OF FAME.

"The garden-land of fame lies between Walhalla and the sea."
                                          SCANDINAVIAN POET.

WOULDST thou walk in the garden of fame,
   Wouldst thou taste of the fruits that grow
In alleys where grapes hang low,
In fields that are never the same?

By the feet of the awful sea
Alone canst thou reach those flowers,
And sit in the shaded bowers,
Calm home of the bird and the bee.

No pathway, no compass can lead,
Alone must thou find the shore,
Alone through the fret and the roar,
Where the mailëd waters tread.

But he who would cling to a spar,
Or hold by a knotted rope,
And laugh in his secret hope,
Nor question his way of a star, —

THE GARDEN OF FAME.

May be saved by a master-hand,
And fast to the shore may hold;
He may see the apples of gold,
He may wander indeed on that strand,

But when the days are fulfilled,
And the master's feet are led
Where only the gods may tread,
And whither the gods have willed, —

Then he who clung to the keel,
Nor worshiped in labor and love,
Nor yearned for the apples, nor strove
With a yearning the lover must feel, —

Sees the waves of oblivion rise
And gather to drag him down;
While the face of the east wears a frown,
And are vanished the god-like eyes.

IN MEMORIAM.

OTTO DRESEL,

July, 1890.

LISTEN, whence come these chords!
    The mighty east blossoms and now is red,
And now the strings of the great harp of light
Are laid across the world, and what was dead
Now newly wakes and sings.

We cannot hear the music where it rings;
We cannot know the words;
But on the sea of harmony there floats,
Forever listening, one who heard the notes
And bore them in his breast
To the sad hearts of men.

Down the far west,
Beyond the space where late the night-bird wings,
Has sunk the leader of our harmonies.
The gardens of the blest

Must vibrate now to antique melodies,
Since he is hither sped;
He heard them in the morning of the world,
And brought them to us down the centuries.

What stillness of the earth now he is gone
And this brief day is done!
Staying our feet,
That fain would follow him,
Stands Silence with veiled head;
The inarticulate pines
Still give their sacred signs,
But far away and dim
Their meaning lies,
And he is dead,
The master and interpreter.

MIDNIGHT.

NIGHT, with thy passionless stars!
    Awake and alone with my grief
I hide in thy coolness, thy calm,
    And my heart finds relief.

Cold is your vigil, O stars!
Ye are mirrored in dew and in tears:
The glad watch ye not, ye pass on
    Seeing the grief of the years.

Thou too, Orion, must sink!
Latest thou heardst our farewell;
Again thou bear'st from me my love,
    And no word canst thou tell.

Ah, Night, how swift art thou sped!
For others day brings a new birth:
Oh, take me! for fain would I pass
    With the stars to the bosom of earth.

Not for me is glory of dawn,
The undoing of deeds that are done:
The light I have lost is still lost
    Though I walk in the sun.

A FAR HAVEN.

"For those who stand in the middle of the water, in the formidable stream that has set in, for those overcome by decay and death, I will tell thee of an island, O Kappa." — ORIENTAL BOOKS.

HOIST the sail and bear away!
   Of an island I have heard
Anchored in the star-sown deep,
Whither Love has gone astray.
Long ago he heard the roar
Of breakers falling on the sand
Of some unknown Indian strand,
And with no reluctant word
Sailed away.
In new meadows, by new seas,
We must seek him with the breeze
Blowing from the gates of sleep.
Listen, we may hear him call
Where goldenrod o'ertops the wall,
Or where the moon across the night
Bends her steps.

A FAR HAVEN.

From that island in the sea
We are told of dreamily
By seers of the Orient,
I hear him call:
What powers have ye lent
To these poor ears,
Spirit of Love!
That in perpetual banishment
Live my dark fears?
For oft I seem to rove,
When shadows fall,
Toward that island, that far island of the sea,
Where thou dost dwell;
And over the sea-swell
Comes a glad vision, to the inward sight,
Of what I heard, O Kappa, and told thee.

THE HAUNTS OF POESY.

IF Poesy thou dost love, and seek to guess
    The shadowy coverts where her footsteps roam,
Easy they seem and common; yet how rare!
The bee and squirrel know, though none the less
Many must seek in vain, nor any come
Into the very place, save love and care
And reverence accompany him there.

Sometimes within a little, plumy dell
Where the brown sparrow cools his rapid wing,
And sometimes under apple-boughs entwined,
We say: Surely 't is here she loves to dwell;
When, lo! she seems no longer one fair thing
Chiefly to choose, but everywhere can find
Loveliness suited to her varying mind.

Sacred the dusty paths of life have grown
From her pure presence. Fluttering bird,
Whose song is hidden in my heart, I hear
Thy music now in yonder treetop's crown;

Yet often, often, is my spirit stirred
By thy low melodies when no trees are near,
When days are dark and all the world is drear.

Late do we learn perchance that thou hast brought
Thy lovers by strange paths thy voice to know;
Strange is the peace thou bringest to the heart!
How many desert places hast thou taught
To speak, how bid the summer breeze to blow
While winter-time and I have sat apart
Enchanted by thy voice, drowned in thy siren art!

THE FOLDING.

"There shall be one fold and one shepherd."

WILD bird flying northward, whither thou?
   And vessel bending southward, what thy quest?
Clouds of the east, with sunshine on your brow,
   Whither? and crescent setting in the west?

Still we pursue while the white day is ours;
   The wild bird journeys northward in his strength;
The tender clouds waste in their sunny bowers,
   One shepherd guides and gathers them at length.

Fly swift, ye birds, against the north wind fly,
   And crowd your sail, ye vessels southward bound!
Rest, rest, ye clouds, upon the happy sky!
   Thus nightly in the fold shall all be found.

TIDES.

"I am the beginning and the end, the first and the last."

THE tide ran low, ran very low, ran out;
    Autumn had settled down upon the land;
And Winter's face, the face of death, was sweet,
For there was calm, an end of strife and doubt.
Strange grew the common sky, the wonted strand,
Since here no more our loving eyes could meet,
No more the aching heart and wearied feet
Rest by Love's side and hold his tireless hand.

But one day, walking by the morning sea,
There rose a wave of summer and of youth
That broke resistless through grief's narrow bound,
And wrought life's past and present and to be
Into one marvelous vision of the truth;
The imperishable joy swept in without one sound.

THE SOUL OF THE POET.

UPON the storm-swept beach brown broken weeds
    Lay scattered far abroad, and as he saw
The wild, disordered strand, "Behold the law,"
He cried, "of my sad mind and her dread needs."
But as he wandered there, those fruitless seeds
Were trampled by his feet while quiet lay
His spirit on the waves, and joined their play
Round a far rock where safe the sea-bird breeds;
And then he knew, not like the strand forlorn,
But like the sea his soul her color drew
From heaven, and all the splendors of the morn
And greater glories that with ripeness grew
Were his, and his the calm the evening knew,
And every grace that out of heaven is born.

HOME.

WHY dost thou urge me thus to leave
　　The gray shore and the busy sea,
Before the autumn learns to grieve
　　His vanished ecstasy?

Here blessings fall about our feet,
Boughs, flame-lit, bear our thoughts on high;
Odors and memories mingle sweet
Where Love hath wandered by.

And they, who still would search, still far
And farther oftentimes must go;
Only the voyager to one star
The guiding light can know.

Peace is not here, she is not there;
She dwells with them who seek her not.
Dear love, stay we at home, for fear
We miss her haunted spot.

ROS SOLIS.

"Paracelsus says that the herb called Ros Solis is, at noon and under a burning sun, filled with dew, while the other herbs around it are dry." — BACON.

THOU lowly herb!
    The lesson thou canst teach my heart would learn,
For the road is hot,
The centre of my being a dry spot!
I hurry and I burn,
Till by the wayside here I thee discern,
Where thou dost hold and gather in the curb
Of thy strong breast
One cool, sweet drop,
While I am so opprest.

On my knees I pause
To watch thee cherishing the dew that fell
In the still hour when Heaven blest Earth
With her cool kiss.

In that one hour of bliss
Behold a sacred birth!
What voice can tell
Thy tender history,
Nor wherewithal thou feed'st this mystery,—
Thy spirit's prop?

Show me thy laws!
Was gladness but a toy
Broken with tears and cast away?
Or is this well a token of thy joy,
A coolness in the heat,
A resting-place for weary feet,
A song for those who cannot sing
But turn, as thou hast done,
Even in the burning sun,
The sorrow of a day
Into a grace no joyous dawn can bring!

SACRED PLACES.

"There are four places which the believing man should visit with feelings of reverence and awe." — ORIENTAL BOOKS.

THE Blessed One hath whispered: There are four
    Places most sacred to believing hearts:
First, where the mother's love her Man-child bore,
And watched his little ways and childish arts.

And one, the second, where the Man-child rose
To know the Holy Spirit dwells within
This casement of the body, and he chose
To hold his breathing temple free from sin.

The third, perchance a narrow plot, whereon
The Man-child stood and served his fellow-men,
And loved the service better than a throne,
And where the suffering world loved him again.

Another, and the fourth, a spot how fair!
Wherefrom the dear one vanished; there the leaves
Lie thick and cover much, but the bright air
Forever tells 't is only earth that grieves.

KYPRIS.

> "O Kypris, daughter of Dione, from mortal to immortal, so men tell, thou hast changed Berenice, dropping softly into the woman's breast the stuff of immortality." — THEOCRITUS.

WHAT hast thou done, Kypris?
    Thou hast pressed thy lip against the cheek
Of that girl sleeping!
Didst thou think, when creeping
To her fair side, of what thy fatal kiss
Could do to that fair creature?
Didst thou wreak
Thy antique vengeance on her,
Thus to review
The shadows and the sorrow Ilium knew?
She was so fair a being, and she wore
Her mortal sweetness with such girlish grace
As when the slender birch in early spring,
Or the June rose in her brief flowering,
We see and stand in silence for a space.

And, now this loveliness hath changed her feature,
The same no more!
Nor time nor space
Hold her in thrall.
Now, gazing on the temples of the sky,
She wanders, lost in thought above,
This little earth (our all),
Dowered with love,
Born into joy of immortality.
What hast thou done, O Kypris!
"A mere kiss,"
Thou sayest.   Yes!

TO THE CHILDREN.

Hunters ever shall ye be,
    Seeking what ye cannot see;
Over hill and over dale,
Through the deepest, greenest vale;
Sure some treasure will be found
Fairer than of common ground.

Fear no wave where thou must cross,
Fear no path of grief or loss:
Through the mist and through the dark
Comes the dawn and sings the lark;
Thus alone ye seek and find
Heaven that never lies behind.

MORTALITY.

THERE is one cup earth's children all may drink;
    One instant full of joy! He seized and drank;
When suddenly, as vessels full-sailed sink,
Struck by the storm, even thus the goblet sank
Out of his keeping, and he backward sank
Into the desert, like to die athirst,
Though longing still to hear the music burst
From other lips, of joy to him a blank.

He was alone! His solitary cry
Returned to him! All voices else were still;
But through the silence of the summer sky
There fell the calmness of eternity, —
There fell the little leaves that drop and die
And hide from sight all sign of mortal ill.

PERMANENCE.

"The beautiful shall be made permanent."
                               KIRKE WHITE.

WHITHER, sweet days?
　　Whither, O Summer?
Whither, O waning moon?
And thou, dear life, belovëd one,
Whither art thou gone?
Not to oblivion!
No wingëd comer,
Wending his skyey ways,
And flown, how soon!
Hath vanished utterly,
Something of Mother Earth,
Something of memory,
Causeth new birth.

Ever undying we pass;
And what man is,
So shall he live though faded with the grass:
If his aim he miss,

And pass unknown — half seen —
Through time's dark screen,
Whatever there may be
Of wingëd life in his endeavor,
This shall be his;
So dowered shall he rise,
Thus painted on the forehead of the skies.

THE WARDER.

TO I. S.

HALF faint with toil from morn to set of sun,
    I watched the shadows creep
Up with slow footstep, when the day was done,
    Toward my encastled steep.

The palace gleamed upon my dazzled sight;
    My heritage was fair;
That night I dreamed my feet were mounting light
    Over the golden stair.

Once more I heard the voice of waters low,
    By perfumed breezes fed;
Methought I followed a grand leader, slow
    Through marble galleries led.

Then sad I wakened in the vale, but found
    My guide still drew me on;
Her name was Charity, her voice a sound
    Of pure compassion.

"Ascend," she said, "to thy fair palace towers;
    Share thou their plenitude!
Thus shalt thou gather with thy growing powers
    Joy to infinitude.

Self whispered suddenly, Where, then, thy home?
    What haunt, what mansion wide?
What refuge after toil in which to roam
    Where silence may abide?

My guide made answer: "Rest is not for thee
    While human hearts must weep:
Go east, go west, in blessing be thou blest,
    Thus thine own heart shall sleep."

Once more the palace gleamed upon my sight;
    Estrangement made it fair;
That night I dreamed my feet were mounting light
    Over the golden stair.

ON THE DEATH OF A YOUNG GIRL.

TRANSLATION FROM THE FRENCH OF PARNY.

SHE leaped out of infancy's arm
   Running over with innocent charm,
And wearing the features of love.
Spared days or but hours from her doom,
This heart, pure as blue skies above,
Had ripened to fragrance and bloom;
But Heaven had destined for death
The allurements of this gentle breath,
And Heaven her life doth now keep
Who sweetly hath fallen on sleep,
Nor murmured against the All-Good.
Even so a smile is effaced;
So dies, nor can ever be traced,
The song of a bird in the wood.

THE PASSING OF TENNYSON.
OCTOBER, 1892.

In the season of the waning moon.

THE king of song is dying while the moon
Sinks pale into illimitable space,
And the great Dawn stretches her golden wings
Once more about the world, as when Love cries,
"Be comforted, thy heart shall no more fret."

Another day! the forehead of the dawn
Wears yet the crescent of the failing moon,
And the dark figure of the shaded whole
Rests, ghost-like, fainting on the slender horns.
Stay with us, O thou ghost! for thou hast seen
His spirit on the wing, and while thou stayest
We cannot quite forget to question thee
Of the great singer in his happier sphere.

Again the day! again the splendid east!
The crescent and the star and the dim dawn
Conspire in silence; and withdraw them hence
Into his unseen land where none may die.

COMATAS.

"And he shall sing how, once upon a time, the great chest prisoned the living goatherd by his lord's infatuate and evil will, and how the blunt-faced bees, as they came up from the meadow to the fragrant cedar-chest, fed him with food of tender flowers because the Muse still dropped sweet nectar on his lips." — THEOCRITUS.

LYING in thy cedarn chest,
 Didst thou think thy singing done,
Comatas? and thyself unblest
 Prisoned there from sun to sun?

Through the fields thy blunt-faced bees
 Sought thy flowers far and away,
And gathered honey from thy trees,
 Thou a prisoner night and day.

Heavy, then, with honeyed store,
 Seeking west and seeking east,
Thee, whose absence they deplore,
 Late they found and brought their feast.

Grief no more shall still thy song,
   Loss, privation, fortune dire!
Servants of air around thee throng
   And touch thy singing lips with fire.

Love, art thou discomforted
   In thy narrow lot to lie?
See! divinely thou art fed
   By the creatures of the sky!

A FALLING STAR.

BEHOLD, she said, a falling star!
    I followed where her vision led,
And saw no meteor near or far,
So swiftly sank the lustre dead.

In silvery moonlight stood she there,
Whiter than silver gleamed her hand,
And gleaming shone her yellow hair,
While dusky shadows filled the land.

She seemed a slender flickering shape,
Framed in the blackness of the porch:
How should a child of night escape,
A foolish moth that loves the torch!

Out of my dusk I came to her;
Voices were stilled anear, afar;
I stood there lost, her worshiper:
She only saw the falling star.

THE POET'S HOUSE.

"For lamentation may not be in a poet's house. Such things befit not us." — SAPPHO.

"Ye shall have a song, as in the night when a holy solemnity is kept, and gladness of heart as when one goeth with a hope into the mountain of the Lord." — ISAIAH.

BESIDE the Indian seas,
   Hid in a sloping vale,
Candulla dwelt, a maid,
White as a wandering sail
That yields now to the breeze,
Now poises, unafraid.

The yellow primrose stands
Thus at the hour of even,
And thus to raise her hands
Seems in the face of heaven;
And so uplifts her eye
When the night of love draws nigh.

Candulla rose and passed
Pure to her lover's home,
A poet's perfect flower
Into his garden come;
But the blossoming day was the last, —
She faded there in the bower; —

And the poet stood alone!
There was silence on the stair,
There was stillness in the hall,
There was absence everywhere!
The summer of life was done,
She had vanished, his love, his all.

He saw her glimmering dress
Wave where the breezes blew,
And where the lilies shone
Her flying feet he knew;
And hers was all the loveliness,
The music hers alone.

Therefore the poet said:
"Stand open, O my door!
And bid the sun illume
Thy sorrow-darkened floor;

Bring garlands for the maid;
The song of life resume."

A sound of gladness and song
Came from his opened door,
As of one who journeys in hope
Where love has traveled before,
And rejoices and is strong
In his joy forevermore.

Voices solemn and sweet,
Children laughing and gay,
Light and purpose of life,
Dawn and falling of May;
The garland of day replete
With flowers that cover the strife, —

Such is the poet's home!
Open the doors to the sun,
Gladness and glory and song,
Till the day of travel be done,
And the day of the Lord be come!
Garlands and song to the children of love belong.

TO ———, SLEEPING.

BELOVËD, when I saw thee sleeping there,
    And watched the tender curving of thy mouth,
The cheek, our home of kisses, the soft hair,
And over all a languor of the south;
And marked thy house of thought, thy forehead, where
All trouble of the earth was then at rest;
And thy dear eyes, a blessing to the blest,
Their ivory gates closed on this world of care, —

Then, then I prayed that never wrong of mine,
That never pain which haunts these earth-built bowers,
If I could hinder, or could aught relieve,
Should ever more make sad this heart of thine;
And yet, dear love, how oft thou leav'st thy flowers,
Here in the rain to walk with me and grieve!

THE MYSTERIES OF ELEUSIS.

SLOWLY, with day's dying fall,
    And with many a solemn sound,
Slowly from the Athenian wall
The long procession wound.

Five days of the mystic nine,
Clad in solemn thought, were passed,
Ere the few could drink the wine
Or seek the height at last.

Then the chosen, young and old,
To Eleusis went their ways;
But no lip the tale has told
Of those mysterious days.

In the seer's hollow eye,
In the maiden's faithful soul,
In youth who did not fear to die,
Men saw that strange control.

Yet no voice the dreadful word,
Through these centuries of man,
Has made the sacred secret heard,
Or showed the hidden plan.

All the horrors born of death
Rose within that nine days' gloom,
Chasing forms of mortal breath
From awful room to room.

Deep through bowels of the earth
Fled those seekers of the dark,
Hearts that sought to find the birth
Of man's immortal spark.

In that moment of despair
Was revealed . . . But who may tell
How the Omnipotent declares
His truth that all is well?

Saw they forms of their own lost?
Heard they voices that have fled?
We know not, or know at most
Their joy was no more dead.

Light of resurrection gleamed,
In what shape we cannot hear;
Glory shone of the redeemed
Beyond this world of fear.

Old books say Demeter came
And smiled upon them, and her smile
Burned all their sorrow in its flame,
Yet left them here awhile.

Mother of the shadowed sphere,
Where we dwell and suffer now,
Lo! the initiate days are here,
Bright is thy dawn-lit brow.

REVERY OF ROSAMOND IN HER BOWER.

DEDICATED TO W. J. W., AFTER HIS SINGING.

THERE came strange days of idlesse, when she said:
"I will recall my rose-days overblown,
The glad, bright sweetness, now forever flown,
That make a queen still queen though she were dead.

"One was at evening, when I heard a voice
Singing of love, of victory, of death,
And all were one; the same delicious breath
Sang victory, love, and death, nor made a choice.

"And now I dwell within a mystic world
Where his voice follows me from dawn to night;
High in my bower imprisoned I watch the light
That ever seems in wings of music furled.

"And when I try to tell what else may be
Of joy for me in memory, still I hear
The singer, nor for love nor death appear
Nor victory, his choice; he sang of three.

"O singer, still thou singest to my heart!
And love and death are now to me as one
Great song forever; surely thou hast won
Indeed a victory, for they cannot part!"

C. T.

BELOVËD, on the shore of this gray world
  Thy little bird, the sandpiper, and I
Now stand alone;
And when mine eye
Returned from following thy upward flight,
And found him here, and heard his tone,
And saw the tiny wing unfurled,
(As oft for thee,)
I knew thy messenger, — 't was he!

His little cry
Is meek and full of joy in things that lie
Close to our feet;
He speeds along the sands, bidding my sight
Grow keen as thine.
He cries, "O love complete,
Thou hast become the leaf and flower
That whisper now companionship;
Oh follow, follow,
Traveller mine!

Thou, too, shalt slip
Into the hand's-breadth hollow
Thy dust shall claim!
And no fair fame
Shall stead thee when the winds of life shall fall;
Only my call
To the unknown, untried, whither these wings
Now vanish: the fading bower
Can hold and soothe thee not!
Oh follow, follow,
'T is Love who sings!
Love, Love is here and beckons thee away;
My song leads on, thou canst not go astray!

THE CORONAL.

"The only prize given to the conqueror was a garland of wild olive."
— History of Greece.

Twine the wild olive, twine!
   And hasten, maidens, while the dayspring calls,
     For when the sun is high
The leaflet droops and falls.

Now the dark hollow seek,
And hide the finished wreath in green recess,
     And droop not, olive leaves,
Nor lose your comeliness.

Hear ye a people's feet
Come trampling up the steep of Athens' hill?
     They bear a sacred gift;
At last the air is still.

Behold the white-robed band,
Holding the mightiest tribute Greece can give, —
     A little fading wreath!
The deed with Zeus shall live.

What needs he other gift,
The hero, with his living torch aflame,
    Held high until the hour
The godhead gild his name!

No dusty sign for him,
No flaunting pile to quicken Fortune's wheel!
    Only Demeter's leaf
And tears that downward steal.

Haste! haste! bring olive!
A people's tribute for the people's hour!
    The gods themselves decree
To give the immortal dower.

THE TRAVELER.

O SORROW! thou that cuttest down the plant
   Of this world's promise close to the very root,
Give us, for lo thou canst! the thing we want, —
Courage, and power above death's mark to shoot.

Come, Sorrow! put thy sweet arms round my neck,
For none are left to do this, only thou;
And thou alone canst help this chain to break
Which binds and will not let me lift my brow!

Thou hast unveiled to me an hour to come, —
How near, how far, thou wouldst not have me know, —
An hour of dawn! but first these feet must roam,
And cross yon mountain-tops grown white with snow.

UPON A MASK OF AN UNKNOWN WOMAN'S FACE.

"L'amor che mi fa bella.'
PARADISO.

WHO is she? The air replies
What know we of name or fame?
Born out of the unknown skies
This fair being came;
But the features of her face,
Where the living story stands,
Tell of no far-distant lands,
No faery dwelling-place.
Other beauty earth shall see
Coming, going with the hour,
Other light shall burn and be
Star of home and dower;
But when spring-time's joy is done,
When the waves their secret keep,
When, the battle lost or won,
We have passed in sleep,

Still thy face, O tender soul!
Shall wear the love of those who weep,
Wear the peace that fills the whole
Of the boundless deep.
Of thy heart we need not ask,
Wert thou joyous? wert thou sad?
White and still beneath this mask,
Spirit of life! thy heart is glad.

"STILL IN THY LOVE I TRUST."

STILL in thy love I trust,
    Supreme o'er death, since deathless is thy essence;
For, putting off the dust,
Thou hast but blest me with a nearer presence.

And so, for this, for all,
I breathe no selfish plaint, no faithless chiding,
On me the snowflakes fall,
But thou hast gained a summer all-abiding.

Striking a plaintive string,
Like some poor harper at a palace portal,
I wait without and sing,
While those I love glide in and dwell immortal.

THE RIVER CHARLES.

BESIDE thee, O my river, where I wait
  Through vista long of years and drink my fill
Of beauty and of light, a steady rill
Of never-failing good, whate'er my state, —

How speechless seem these lips, my soul how dull,
Never to say, nor half to say, how dear
The washing of thy ripples, nor the full
And silent flow which speaks not to the ear!

Thou hast been unto me a gracious nurse,
Telling me many a tale in listening hours
Of those who praised thee with their ripening powers,
Our elder poets, nourished at thy source.

O happy Cambridge meadows! where now rest
Forever the proud memories of their lives;
O happy Cambridge air! forever blest
With deathless song the bee of time still hives; —

And farther on, where many a wildflower blooms
Through a fair Sunday up and down thy banks,
Beautiful with thy blossoms, ranks on ranks,
What vanished eyes have sought thy dewy rooms!

I, too, have known thee, rushing, bright with foam,
Or sleeping idly, even as thou dost now,
Reflecting every wall and tower and dome,
And every vessel, clear from stern to prow.

Or in the moonlight, when the night is pale,
And the great city is still, and only thou
Givest me sign of life, and on thy brow
A beauty evanescent, flitting, frail!

O river! ever drifting toward the sea,
How common is thy fate! thus purposeless
To drift away, nor think what 't is to be,
And sink in the vast wave of nothingness.

But ever to love's life a second life
Is given, and his narrow river of days
Shall flow through other lives, and sleep in bays
Of quiet thought and calm the heart at strife.

Fortunate river! that through the poet's thought
Hast run and washed life's burden from his sight;
O happy river! thou his song hast brought,
And thou shalt live in poetry and light.

FLAMMANTIS MŒNIA MUNDI.

I STOOD alone in purple space and saw
    The burning walls of the world, like wings of flame,
Circling the sphere: there was no break nor flaw
In those vast airy battlements whence came
The spirits who had done with time and fame
And all the playthings of earth's little hour;
I saw them each, I knew them for the same,
Mothers and brothers and the sons of power.

Yet were they changed; the flaming walls had burned
Their perishable selves, and there remained
Only the pure white vision of the soul,
The mortal part consumed, and swift returned
Ashes to ashes; while unscathed, unstained,
The immortal passed beyond the earth's control.

"A THOUSAND YEARS IN THY SIGHT ARE BUT AS ONE DAY."

NEITHER joy nor sorrow move
    The figure at the feet of Love;
Light of breathing life is she,
Spirit of immortality.

Lead me up thy stony stair,
O Spirit, into thy great air!
For his day of pain and tears
Is to man a thousand years.

DEATH, WHO ART THOU?

THUS questioned they who watched the Ægean Sea
    Stretch up white arms to drag the diver down,
And they who waked to find Thermopylæ
    Scarlet and white with glory overblown.

Tears dropped, even then, in that far early world, —
    Dropped on the soft face of the fresh-turned earth;
And curses gathered by despair were hurled
    By mortal sorrow in her primal birth.

But the young runner grasped his wreath and died;
    Antinous loved and plunged him in the deep;
The goal attained, — world's glory and world's pride, —
    Life held no more, they said, and sank to sleep.

Death, thou wert laurel and crown in that young dawn;
    Happy the heroes in thy dusky fields

With double flute and forms in ghostly lawn
   Dancing, or bearing calm their shadowy shields.

Ages rolled on, a mighty Teacher came;
   The words He spake were spirit and were life;
The hearts of men kindled and were aflame;
   Sudden he vanished, leaving them at strife.

Yet He had said: "The things that now I know
   The world knows not; hereafter this shall be;
Proof of my love and faith, behold I go
   Fearless away, whither men cannot see."

Then in the dark they questioned yet again
   After his light went out: "Behold the pit!
Thither the Master went through blood and pain
   Into the silence. Let us worship it!"

Yet ever through the darkness came one ray,
   The Master's birth-star glimmering in the east;
And they who watched, they also learned to pray
   For clearer vision and for light increased.

Again the ages pass, and still they find
  On woodland pathways lovers two by two,
Held by the ties which mortal creatures bind
  To last forever, ever seeming new.

Yet autumns must return, and leave beside
  The dying embers one who sits alone,
Crying, "Oh, where? What planet calls thy tide
  While I remain to know the summer done?"

"Still am I here," Love answers; "time is short
  And life is endless, and the spirit mounts!
The little good I strove for, and what wrought,
  Was but a child's task that the man recounts.

"You question what is death? Behold the tide
  That bore me swiftly from you hither brought
All but the frail frame in the earth's green side,
  And quickens in the flow the living thought.

"And I would tell thee more"— Then stillness fell
  Abroad upon the earth; voice there was none.
Alas! the voice of Love can no more tell!
  But Death will show that Love and he are one.

The Publishers of Harper's Magazine, of the Century Magazine, of Scribner's Magazine, and the Atlantic Monthly have kindly allowed the republication in this volume of such poems as have been printed in their pages.

www.ingramcontent.com/pod-product-compliance
Lightning Source LLC
Chambersburg PA
CBHW030253170426
43202CB00009B/722